SKIING

A SKIER'S DICTIONARY

skiing

A SKIER'S DICTIONARY

BY HENRY BEARD
& ROY McKIE

METHUEN

Original edition published in the United States of America in 1989
by Workman Publishing Company, New York

This revised edition first published in Great Britain in 1991
by Methuen, Michelin House, 81 Fulham Road, London SW3 6RB

ISBN 0 413 66280 2
A CIP catalogue record for this book is available from the British Library

Printed in Great Britain
by St Edmundsbury Press Ltd, Bury St Edmunds, Suffolk

To all those who have heard the call of the slopes.

Alp

A

Aerials	Competitive form of ski jumping in which daredevil skiers attempt various midair acrobatics such as somersaults, back flips and body twists. Points are awarded on the basis of the length of the hospital stay, the size of the bill, the originality of the X-rays, the degree of difficulty of the surgery, and the creativity displayed in filling out the insurance claim as measured by the speed and size of payment. *See* HOTDOGGING.
Alp	*1.* One of a number of ski mountains in Europe. *2.* A shouted request for assistance made by a skier. An appropriate reply is "What's Zermatter?"
Alpine	The formal descriptive term for downhill skiing, one of the four basic ski techniques. The other three are nordic (cross-country skiing), norpine (downhill skiing on cross-country equipment), and asinine (snowboarding).
Altitude Sickness	In addition to the common symptoms of headache, dizziness, vertigo, nausea, and insomnia, subtler physical conditions brought on by breathing the oxygen-poor atmosphere at high-altitude ski resorts include a love of being cold (Nansen's Disease), an indifference to heights (the Icarus Complex), a compulsion to apply wax to things (Tussaud's Complaint), an impulse to wear ugly or silly clothing (The Wally Syndrome), and an urge to immediately dispose of any excess cash (Alpine Ski Shop Fever).
American Teaching Method	A simplified, accelerated system of ski instruction in which students are taught how to jump the lift queue before they learn the snowplough.

Angulation	The ideal balanced posture for standing on or traversing a slope, in which the hips and knees are thrust inward toward the hill while the head and torso are angled outward and downhill in a smooth curve often called the "comma position". A more usual posture is one in which the skier's entire body is tilted away from the down slope and into the hill, the skier ends up with his arms out and skis askew in the "asterisk" position.
Anticipation	The first of six basic phases of the classic ski turn. It is followed by Initiation, Trepidation, Desperation, Exclamation, and Recuperation. *See* TURN.
Après-ski	Descriptive term for activities in a ski resort in the evening following a day on the slopes. Typical of these are le bitch and la moan, le stiff drink, le soaking des tootsies, le long nap, le big wait at le expensive dump for la dreadful meal, beaucoup de wondering why le hell we do this stuff, and le checking on la airline to see if they have le earlier flight home.
Artificial Snow	Man-made snow produced by forcing a jet of water or an air-and-water mixture out of a nozzle under very high pressure. The snowmaking process creates a slope surface indistinguishable from a real snowfall in all but one respect: even the lightest sleepers at a ski resort generally will not sit bolt upright in bed at 5:00 A.M. if a couple of inches of natural snow begin to fall.
Avalanche	One of the very small number of actual perils that skiers face and that needlessly frighten timid individuals away from the sport. *See also* BLIZZARD, CONTUSION, FRACTURE, FROSTBITE, GONDOLA PLUNGE, HYPOTHERMIA, LIFT COLLAPSE, POLE PUNCTURE, SNOWMOBILE MISHAP, WHITEOUT, and YETI.

Après-ski

Big Foot

B

Bare Spot	A place where, due to insufficient snowfall, the underlying earth is visible. Depending on weather conditions, bare spots can range from a patch the size of a footprint to a patch the size of the French Alps.
Base	*1.* The layer of plastic on the bottom of a ski that is no longer there because *2.* The layer of snow on the surface of a slope is no longer there.
Bastard	*1.* A wide, flat, single-cut file used to flatten and sharpen ski edges. *2.* Someone who charged you for hand-filing your ski edges but used a belt-sander instead.
Belt Bag	A small zip-up bag, sometimes also called a purse belt, which is attached to the waist by a belt and positioned just above the rump. It is a superb shock absorber for bruising backward falls since it is usually filled with a dense, pasty, body-cushioning substance made of suntan lotion that has leaked from the tube, crushed Mars bars, a wad of sticky money, and a burst packet of hand-warmer fluid.
Bent Ski Poles	*1.* Expert skiers' poles shaped at the factory to fit around the body and thus reduce wind resistance. *2.* Beginning skiers' poles shaped during use to fit around trees, trail signs, and chairlift pylons.
Big Foot	Giant, hairy-bodied reclusive humanoid said to live in remote mountain areas. Such creatures probably do not exist, but if they do and they ever decide to take up skiing, they're in luck because ski-equipment rental shops have a remarkably large selection of boots that appear to have been designed for their exclusive use.

Bindings

Ingenious automatic mechanisms that attach the skis to the ski boots at the heel and toe. Bindings very effectively protect skiers from potentially serious injury during a bad fall by releasing the ski from the boot, sending it skittering across the slope where it trips another skier, who avoids serious injury when his bindings release, allowing his skis to spring loose and trip two other skiers, who fall, causing their bindings to release before they suffer serious injury, sending their skis into the path of four other skiers, and so on, eventually causing the entire slope to be closed, thus protecting every skier in the area from serious injury.

Bones

There are 206 bones in the human body. While this statement of potential vulnerability may dismay some skiers, particularly novices, it is worth noting that according to medical records two of them, the left and right stapes of the inner ears, have never been broken in any reported skiing accident.

Boogy

To ski flat out; one of several terms that surfing has contributed to skiing. Skiing terms, however, have not found their way to the beach, partly because of the lack of appeal of the basic "schusser" look (a runny nose, chapped lips, and a major limb in a cast) and partly because the Franco-German sources of most skiing expressions have poor substitutes for such pithy, snappy terms as "bummer" (Oh, dîtes-donc, quel grand malheur), "far out" (Träumerisch), "hot dog" (Bockwurst), "cool" (bien refraîchisse), "go for it" (allez, faîtes la tentative), "cruising" (la grande descente dans le style de la croisière), and "wipe-out" (Ausradierung).

Boot

See PAIN.

Camber

Boot Fit

1. The extent to which a ski boot is the right size or shape for a foot. *2.* A highly emotional outburst caused by wearing ski boots that are the wrong size or shape.

Bump

1. A swelling resulting from *2.* A blow caused by tripping over *3.* An elevated mound of snow. *See* MOGUL.

C

Cable Car

An aerial tramway consisting of heavy, pylon-supported cables strung very far above the ground from which is suspended a large cabin capable of carrying over a hundred skiers on a fast, steep ascent to a high-altitude skiing area. It is also known as the Téléférique, the Horroférique, or the Petriférique.

Camber

A built-in arch or convexity found in all skis, varying in depth of curve among different models and manufacturers. Other areas of variation in ski design include "side-cut," the degree of taper in the waist; "splay," the steepness of curve of the tip; "flex," the amount of torsional movement in the body of the ski; "damping," the ability of the ski to limit vibration; "swingweight," the weight distribution over the ski's length; "repellence," the ugliness of colouration, trade-marks, and designs on the top of the ski' "shameface," the degree of embarrassment caused by the cheapness of the ski; "flingstrength," the ski's resistance to mishandling by airline personnel; "scathe," the rate of deterioration of the ski when dumped in a hall cupboard; "swipe-risk," the ski's desirability to a thief; and "searchlength," the amount of time its owner would spend looking for it in deep snow at the edge of the piste at 4 o'clock on a Sunday afternoon.

Carrying Skis   Even when held tightly together by straps or interlocking brakes, a pair of skis is awkward to manage. To master the knack of carrying them, ask a friend to stand close behind you on your right or left side. Place the skis over your shoulder, with the tips forward and the bindings just touching your back, and drape your arm over their top surface. Now pivot on your hips slowly in both directions as if looking at the scenery. The last foot or so of your skis should hit your friend smartly at about ear level. If you're grazing the top of his head or just nudging him somewhere around his belt, adjust your grip, increase the speed of your hip turn, or flatten the slope of the ski-carrying angle.

Carved Turn   A high-speed skidless parallel turn made with minimum body movement; the aspiration of obsessive skiers.

Cast   A high-strength rigid plaster dressing designed for minimum body movement; the destination of obsessive skiers.

Catching an Edge   Accidentally letting the edge of a ski dig into the snow; one of the 640 most common causes of falls in skiing.

Chairlift   A transportation system in which a series of chairs suspended from a cable rapidly conveys 1, 2, 3, or 4 skiers at a time from the front of one lift queue to the rear of another.

Check   A traversing manoeuvre in which skiers reduce speed on a steep hill by setting the edge of their skis into the snow, then head into the next turn with a bouncing motion.

Cheque   A financial manoeuvre in which skiers reduce expenses at a ski resort with steep prices by slapping an oblong piece of paper on the cashier's desk, then head for the airport before it makes a bouncing motion.

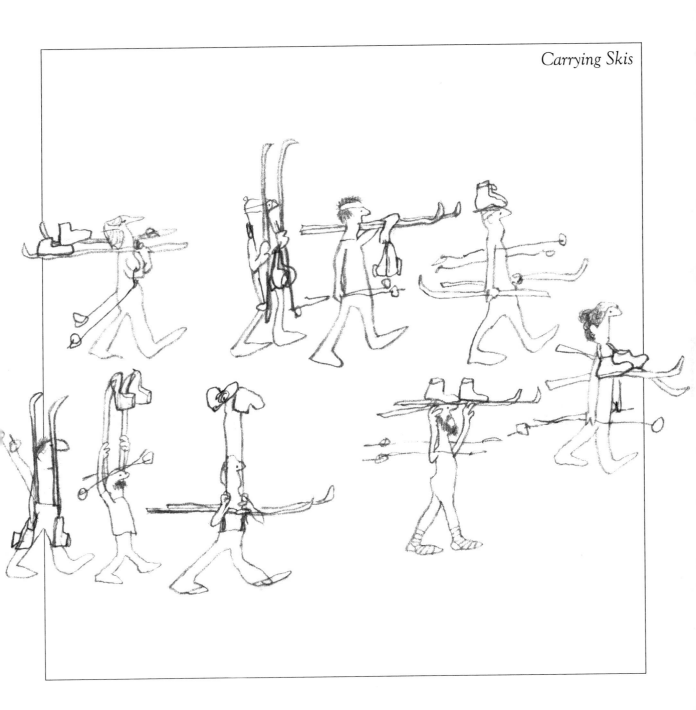

Compound Fracture

Christie

Term for any skidded turn that ends with the skis in a parallel position. The manoeuvre was introduced and perfected by Norwegians who named it for Norway's capital city, Christiania, from which it was eventually contracted to "christie." In 1925, reacting to a wave of public revulsion at the perversion of pure nordic skiing technique by downhill-crazed foreigners who were experimenting with such horrors as the stem Christiania and the scissor Christiania, Norway's parliament, the Storting, voted to change the name of the capital to something completely unrelated to the new so-called sport of alpine skiing. Oslo was the final choice, but interestingly, on the long list of runners-up were Lippbålm, Velkrø, Däyglö, Måmbo, Pømä, and Demö, and Tåhøe, Altå, Äspenn, and Støwe.

Citizen Race

A long-distance race open to amateur nordic skiers. The most famous are the 22-mile Birkebeiner in Norway, and Switzerland's 26-mile Engadine Marathon, but a pair of less well-known, but equally demanding endurance races are growing in popularity: Austria's Baggageblunder, in which skiers using ill-fitting rental equipment ski a 12-mile circuit around Innsbruck airport looking for their luggage, and France's 32-mile Savoie Carathon, in which teams of cross country skiers tow disabled Citroens from a carpark in Alpe d'Huez to a garage on the outskirts of Grenoble.

Code

1. A set of rules governing how a skier should behave on the slopes. *2.* A stuffed-up node that a skier cad get from staddig aroud id wet clode id a lift queue.

Compound Fracture

One of the two worst things that someone can end up with in a ski area.

Condo

The other.

Convenience Boot	Term for a rear-entry design alpine ski boot which has an internal cable system that makes it possible for a skier to produce total discomfort over the entire foot with a single preset lever.
Conventional Boot	Term for a front-entry design alpine ski boot which has a number of micro-adjustable buckles that make it possible for a skier to produce a welt, bruise, blister, or pinch at any desired point on the foot.
Cross-country Skiing	Traditional Scandinavian all-terrain snow-travelling technique. It isn't difficult to learn, nor is it dangerous. It's good exercise, but it isn't strenuous or likely to cause injuries. Its equipment isn't complex, uncomfortable, or particularly expensive. It doesn't require the purchase of costly lift tickets, and it doesn't involve rides on aerial transport devices. It has no crowds or lines. It doesn't attract rich twits or adolescent twerps. Snow bimbos make fun of it. Snowboarders shun it. It isn't skiing. *See* CROSS-COUNTRY SOMETHING-OR-OTHERING.
Cross-country Something-or-othering	Recreational cross-country touring on skis, usually along trails in scenic wilderness areas. More and more skiers have discovered the pleasures of gliding through the silent, peaceful, snow-hushed woods, far from the noise and crowds of the ski slopes, moving with the restful rhythm of the classical nordic step, with no sound but the whispery hiss of the skis slipping through the snow, the soft slapping of the loose backpack flap, the muffled tinkle of the room keys dropping into the puffy powder of a deep, wind-sculpted drift, the sharp, crisp snap of a ski binding breaking, and the eerie wail of elemental rage as man comes to grips with the ancient force of nature.

Destination Resort

D

Daily Snow Report	A printed or broadcast description of the local snow cover at a given ski area based on information provided by its managers. Since slope surfaces can vary considerably, skiers should be familiar with a few common terms used by resorts to describe local conditions: packed powder (wet slush), packed powder (glare ice), packed powder (frozen granules), packed powder (breakable crust), and packed powder (a light dusting of snow on mostly bare earth).
Descent Route	An unmarked, off-piste ski run that should never be attempted by any skier with skis less than 180cm long, a Swiss rating below Class 6, an Austrian rating below Class 1, a French rating below Class 3, or an IQ above 75.
Destination Resort	A full-service skiing facility that offers not just lift queues, but also locker queues, front desk queues, elevator queues, shuttle-bus queues, restaurant queues, and cinema queues.
DIN	Deutsche Industrie-Norm, or German Industrial Standard, a set of internationally accepted standards that includes the settings for ski bindings. A chart produced by German engineers provides for ski shops precise instructions on setting the release point for toe and heel bindings based on the weight, physical structure, and bone strength of individual skiers, their grooming and personal hygiene, their posture while standing at strict attention, their knowledge of the applicable rules and regulations, their overall cooperativeness with the proper authorities, and their readiness at all times to do exactly as they are told without snivelling like the miserable, inferior weaklings they are.

Double Boot	A modern, two-piece ski boot, designed so that the part that won't close correctly is separate from the part that doesn't fit properly. *See* INNER BOOT and OUTER SHELL.
Double-pole Push	A method of crossing flat terrain by propelling oneself forward using both ski poles at the same time. Making this powerful pushing motion is strenuous, but it does help develop the muscles skiers will need at the end of a ski trip to cram 90 pounds of lumpy, puffy ski equipment into a couple of suitcases and still have plenty of upper-arm strength left over to beat their fists in rage on the counters of the hotel front desk, the rental car office, and the airline.
Down	Polite synonyms for the act and result of falling should always be employed. For "down," use "unup" or "formerly perpendicular"; for "to fall," substitute "pronificate," "supinize," or "recumbify"; and instead of "fall," say "snow check," "slope pause," or "whole-body surface contact."
Dry Slope	A hill covered with a plastic or nylon surface to permit skiing in snow-free regions. Dry slopes ski quite realistically and in some areas, injection-moulding equipment may be rented so skiers can make polyvinyl chloride "snowmen".

E

Edging	*1.* Vital skiing skill that involves using a rolling motion of the knees and hips to tilt the ski edges into the slope, making it possible to stand still on the fall line. *2.* Vital skiing skill that involves using a series of hip movements and shoulder turns to thrust the body slowly forward, making it possible to gain several places in the lift queue.

Egg

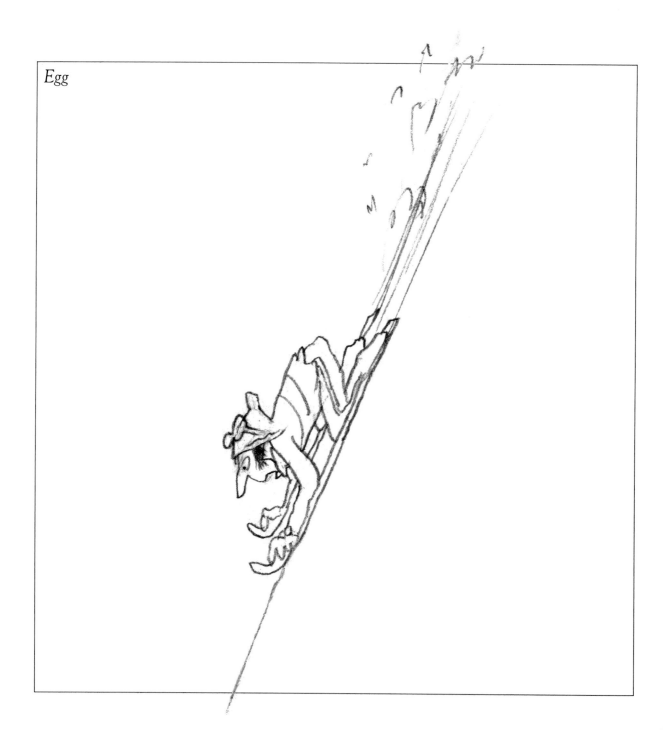

Egg

Name for a crouched or tucked body position used by skiers to eliminate wind resistance on a fast, straight downhill run. It is often followed by the Dropped Egg, the Egg Roll, and the Omelette.

Elasticity

The ability of a ski binding to permit some toe and heel movement before releasing, usually measured in terms of RCT (return to centre time). The other basic measures of a binding's quality are its RSA (how long before it is returned to the shop for adjustment), its TBSS (time before something goes *sproing*), DSBF (days in a shop being fixed) and NTSSASS (number of times skier swears at the salesman who sold it to him).

Exercises

It is important to be in proper physical condition before going skiing. Here are a few simple exercises you can do to make sure you're prepared for the slopes:
- Stand in one place for five minutes, then take two steps forward. Repeat 10 times.
- Attach an anvil to each foot with old belts or rope and walk up and down a flight of stairs.
- Sit on a second-storey window ledge with your skis on and your poles in your lap for 30 minutes.
- Tie your legs together at the ankles and lie flat on the floor; then, holding a banana in each hand, get to your feet.
- Grasp a credit card in your non-writing hand, then sign your name 100 times.

F

Fall

1. A poor season for skiing. *2.* A good reason for not skiing.

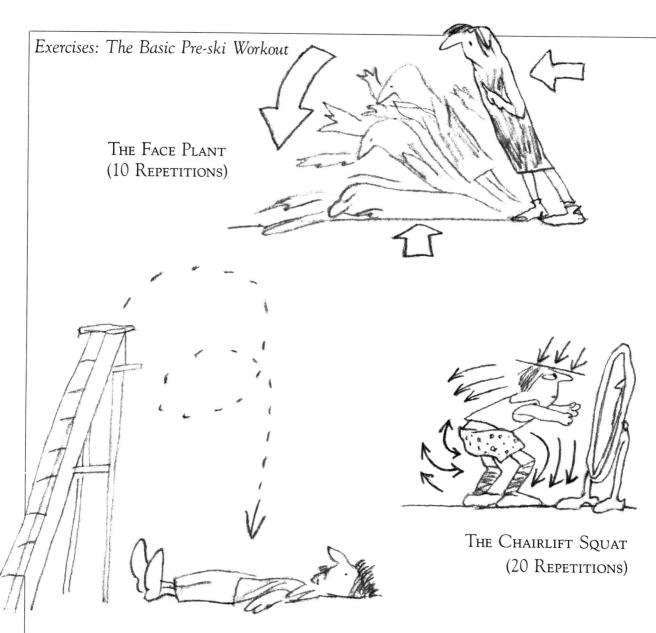

Exercises: The Basic Pre-ski Workout

THE FACE PLANT
(10 REPETITIONS)

THE CHAIRLIFT SQUAT
(20 REPETITIONS)

THE BACK FLOP (5 REPETITIONS)

AEROBIC WORKOUT ON THE SCHUSSCYCLE (15 MINUTES)

Fall Line

An imaginary line following the steepest and most direct path down any given slope. Skiers executing turns and traverses constantly pass across the fall line as they make their way downhill, often stopping for a while at other imaginary boundary marks like the Topple Corridor, the Tumble Lane, the Stagger Path, and the Stumble Zone.

Fear

See ICE.

Finnish Step

1. A cross-country skiing technique used by racers to rest their muscles in which the pole plant is left out on every second or third stride. Also known as the "swinging step" or "triple striding." *2.* A cross-country skiing technique used by skiers who have to go to the lavatory badly in which a series of very short, almost hopping steps are made with the knees held close together. Also known as the "squirming step," "Finnish two-step," or "nordic twitch."

Freestyle Mogul Skiing

A skiing event in which competitors are judged on their speed, style, and control as they race down steep, heavily moguled slopes to the sound of prerecorded music of their choice. For some reason, most "bump skiers" choose the music of the Rolling Stones as accompaniment, particularly the tunes "Shattered," "Twisted," "Please, Doctor, I'm Damaged," and "Let It Bleed."

G

Geländesprung

German term for a daring aerial manoeuvre in which a skier jumps from the edge of a bump, ridge, or slope in order to clear an obstacle by leaping over it. The word is pronounced "godDAMNwhataSTUPIDthingtoDO."

Gloves Skiers' hand coverings that have precisely calibrated thermal layers to provide excessive warmth on hotter days and insufficient heat on colder ones; that are designed to be tight enough around the back of the hand and wrist to restrict circulation but not to be so close-fitting on the fingers as to allow any discernible manual dexterity; that are able to admit moisture from the outside without permitting any dampness within to escape; and that are bulky enough to ensure that they won't fit into any known pocket while still being light enough to be easily knocked or blown off a lap if removed during a ride on a chairlift.

Goggles Eye-protection device that greatly reduces the sun's potentially damaging glare by using a tiny amount of trapped moisture to produce, directly in front of the wearer's eyes, a dense layer of light-absorbing fog.

Gondola A ski lift consisting of a series of small, enclosed, somewhat cramped cabins suspended from a continuously moving overhead cable to which they are engaged by an operator once they are fully loaded. It is a fast and easy way to go up the mountain unless you suffer from acrophobia (fear of heights), claustrophobia (fear of confined spaces), fatsophobia (fear of being sat on by a corpulent person), gabbophobia (fear of having to make conversation with a dolt), velcrophobia (fear of becoming permantly attached to someone else's pocket flap), or autoparkasphyxiaphobia (fear of being smothered by one's own down ski jacket).

Gravity One of the four basic forces that affect skiers. The others are the strong force, which jams their bindings; the weak force, which causes their ankles to wobble; and electromagnetism, which makes their car batteries go dead.

Grip & Glide	The two basic actions of a properly waxed nordic ski.
Gripe & Grouse	The two basic actions of a nordic skier on improperly waxed skis.

H

Hat	Any of several types of soft, insulating headgear worn by skiers. As a rule, skiers do not wear hard-shelled, impact-proof helmets to prevent head injuries. This may be because any individual who believes it's fun descending a steep slope at a high rate of speed on a cold day clearly lacks a vital organ above the neck that requires protection.
Heli-skiing	A form of off-piste skiing in which skiers are transported by helicopter to the summits of remote mountains without ski lifts. Heli-skiing has the advantage of providing pristine, deep-powder slopes and no lift queues, but the absence of facilities does turn some people off, particularly those who are concerned by the problems inherent in heli-going-to-the-bathroom, heli-finding-a-lost-ski, and heli-walking-all-the-way-down while heli-freezing-to-death.
Herringbone	A method for ascending a slope in which a skier plants his skis into the snow with the tails together and the tips apart and climbs with short, duck-walking steps. This manoeuvre can be tiring and time-consuming, but it has its advantages: you never have to look down the mountain, nobody ever wants to race you, you don't need to do anything clever to come to a full stop, and you have at least 20 minutes from the time you first see a tree until the moment you hit it.

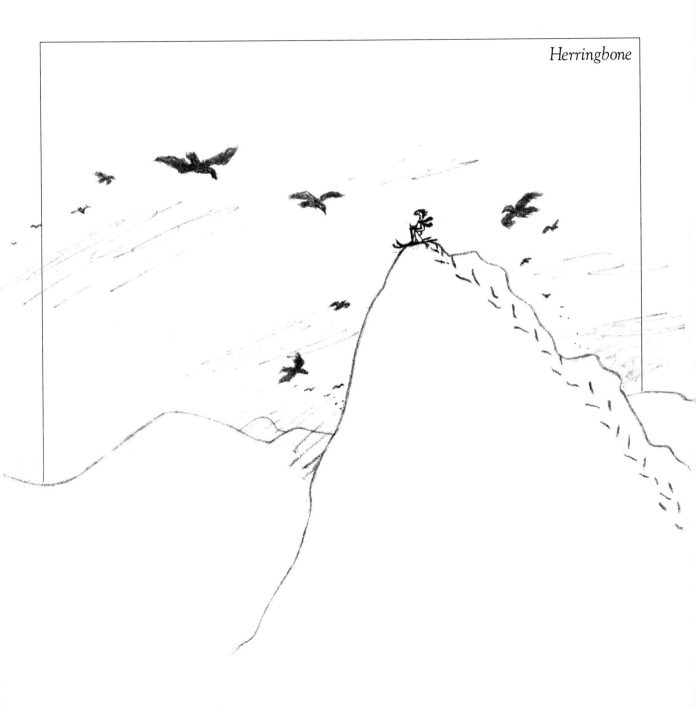

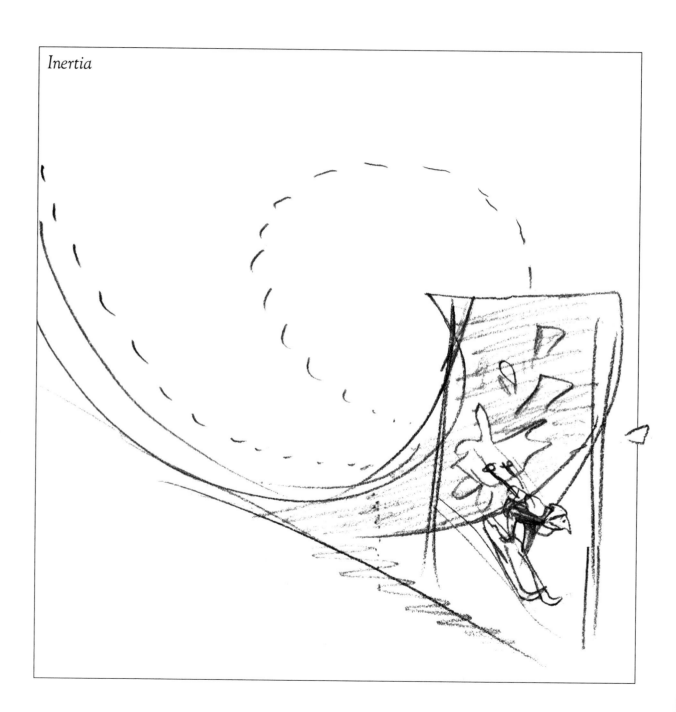

Inertia

Hotdogging	Term for freestyle acrobatic skiing, done on a slope or from a jump on special skis, with demanding aerial movements like the Outrigger, the Backscratcher, the Moebius Flip, the Space Walk, and the Wongbanger. *See* HOTFOOTING.
Hotfooting	Term for freestyle ski-boot walking, done on snow, icy pavement, or stairs while carrying a pair of skis over the shoulder, with demanding terrestrial movements like the Moon Walk, the Gulag Shuffle, the Frankenstein Stomp, the Step Slip, the Pole Trip, and the Shinbanger.
Hoting Ski	The earliest known ski, a short, wide, quite crude and inefficient-looking slab of slightly curved and pointed pine wood with slits for some sort of strap. About 4,500 years old, it was unearthed from a peat bog in Sweden. Only one ski of the pair was found, along with a twisted piece of mangled iron, the equally primitive Hoting Ski Lock.

I

Ice	*See* FEAR.
Inertia	The tendency of a skier's body to resist changes in direction or speed due to the action of Newton's First Law of Motion. Other physical laws that affect skiers include: • Two objects of greatly different mass falling side by side will have the same rate of descent, but the lighter one is going to have larger hospital bills. • Matter can be neither created nor destroyed, but if it drops out of a ski jacket pocket, don't expect to encounter it again in our universe. • No two bodies can occupy precisely the same location at

exactly the same time unless the gondola loader is a true professional.

- It is impossible to reduce the temperature of anything to absolute zero, but if the chairlift you are riding stops halfway uphill, you are going to get very, very close.
- Every action taught by one ski instructor is opposed by an equally qualified ski instructor with an opposite point of view.
- When an irresistible force meets an immovable object, an unethical lawyer will immediately appear.
- Even though there is no such thing as perpetual motion, it is definitely not a good idea to stand still after getting off the chairlift.
- What goes up, must wait.
- A body at rest will continue at rest even after it is acted upon by an outside force unless that force opens the blinds, turns the radio on loud and takes away the covers.

Injury
Physical harm or damage suffered as the result of a skiing accident. Past studies seem to show that injuries are most common on that "one last run of the day" when skiers are tired and their concentration is poor. New evidence suggests, however, that it is when they are incompletely warmed up, overeager, and impulsive that skiers run the greatest risk of suffering a mishap, and that consequently, if they simply eliminate entirely that alluring but potentially disastrous first run of the day, the chance of injury is effectively reduced to zero.

Inner Boot
The soft, pliable interior part of an alpine ski boot, which, if it didn't pinch, would keep the foot, if the right socks had been worn, firmly and comfortably in place if the outer shell didn't bind. *See* OUTER SHELL, SOCK.

Inside Ski

Inside Ski	Term used by instructors for the ski on the inside of any turn which is also the downhill ski at the start of the turn, the uphill ski at the end of the turn, and the outside ski in the next turn. Students refer to it by a more informal term like "the ski that thingees on the whatsis." *See* OUTSIDE SKI.

J

Jacuzzi	Circular therapeutic bathing pool where, after a long day on the slopes, skiers can get into hot water with their loved ones or get into hot water with their loved ones.
Jet Turn	*1.* A turn that is initiated by propelling the feet forward. *2.* A turn that is cancelled because of equipment problems, or is made with an intermediate unplanned stop, or is diverted to an unintended destination.

K

Kick Turn	A technique for making a 180° turn while standing on a slope in which the skier lifts and pivots the skis, one by one, until they are both pointed in the opposite direction from their original position. It's a complicated and awkward manoeuvre, and so most skiers save up all their really sharp stationary turns for a rest stop in the middle or at the end of the day when they can take off their skis and just twirl around a few times on their way to the bathroom.
Kinderski	Common, generic term for a special children's ski school in a resort area. Even very small children learn to ski quickly and easily, but fortunately for the adults whom they leave

behind on the slopes in a cloud of powder, they have much more difficulty mastering other equally important aspects of the skiing experience: for example, they have a great deal of trouble climbing barstools; few of them can fill out a credit card voucher, even with a crayon; none of them knows the difference between pasta and pesto; and most of them would drown in a jacuzzi.

Klister   A thick ski wax that comes out of the tube in a klumsy klotted klump of klinging krud.

Knapsack   A bag used by skiers to carry around a large knumber of things knobody ever ends up kneeding.

L

Layering   Putting on several relatively thin overlapping items of clothing, one over the other, rather than one or two thick, bulky articles. This method not only produces greater warmth, more effective protection against dampness, and superior insulation from the wind, but also increases the odds that in the faddy, fast-changing world of ski styles, something that you're wearing on some part of your body will be in fashion for some portion of your ski trip.

Lift Line   1. A group of people waiting their turn to board a ski lift. 2. An opening remark or observation used in an attempt to start a conversation with an attractive individual in a lift line, such as "You know, I could spot it a mile away—you're an outdoorsy sort of person, aren't you?" or "Isn't that a coincidence—we both seem to be wearing the same number of skis!"

Z

Zdarsky, Mathias A turn-of-the-century Austrian skiing pioneer with an astonishing number of "firsts" to his credit, including being the first person to use the snowplough and stem turns, producing the first study of avalanches, designing the first slalom course, starting the first ski school, developing the first teaching technique (Do it, You stink, Pay me, Go away), writing the first illustrated ski manual ("Ski My Way, You Fool"), and even constructing the first jacuzzi (though his name for it, "The Hell Vat," proved an obstacle to its speedy popularization). Ironically, even in death he was an innovator. He perished in the world's first ski lift accident in 1933, when his ingenious Mountain Zeppelin, a series of chain-linked, cable-driven mini-blimps, exploded. He was buried, according to his wishes, on his beloved ski slopes, on a peak at the end of a funicular railway. Thousands attended his funeral, patiently waiting for their places on the cogwheel train. It was the world's first lift line.